T0342952

AUSTRALIAN COOKING

AUSTRALIA

Introduction

Australians are fortunate in so many ways with the abundance of natural good produce available and the cuisine of cooking comes from various cultures around the world including British, European, Asian and Middle Eastern. And the food industry in Australia is one of the most self-sufficient in the world with daily produce, plenty of supplies of meat, grains, fruit and vegetables along with seafood all year round.

Since the pioneering days meat has been an important part of the Australian diet, with the most popular being grills, barbecues, casseroles and the traditional roast. In Australia we have one of the best reputations in the world for our rural industry which offers excellent quality of beef, our exceptional fat-marbled wagyu, veal, lamb, pork and poultry. Kangaroo is also a great healthy, low fat mild flavoured meat that is available all year round and becoming a staple part of Australia's weekly diet.

With Australia's climate, fresh food is produced all year round and there is very little food that is imported into Australia. We are a nation driven by paddock to plate and while we are a nation of meat eaters, we also indulge in plant based and organic fruits and vegetables.

Most of the Australian population lives along the coastlines so seafood is in abundance and enjoyed by Australians regularly. There are plenty of prawns on offer with many Aussies just eating a bucket of prawns with their favourite sauce on the side or a dozen natural Pacific or Rock oysters. There are also different species of fish around each state's coastline: Barramundi, Snapper, Flathead or John Dory being the most popular fishes to cook and Australians also love the traditional fish and chips that you can buy from the fish and chip shop to eat on a picnic blanket at the beach or somewhere outdoors looking at the water.

The cuisine in Australia is about quality

ingredients and the people on the land that produce it.

In Australia there is also a winemaking culture dating back to the 1800s and there are wine regions in almost all states with the most famous being the Hunter Valley, Clare Valley, The Barossa and Coonawarra, the Yarra Valley and Margaret River and Tasmania's Tamar Valley. There are some of extraordinary wines on offer including the iconic wine, Penfolds Grange, one of the most sought after wines in the world. Not only is there an active wine culture, Australia also has a craft beer boom with breweries and bars popping up around the continent and lastly, not to forget, the gin distilleries.

STARTERS

Prawn Cocktail

250 g prawns cooked and peeled
4 large lettuce leaves, finely shredded
slices of lemon, to garnish

Cocktail sauce

3 tablespoons thick mayonnaise
1 tablespoon tomato ketchup, or thick tomato
purée, or skinned fresh sieved tomatoes
1 tablespoon Worcestershire sauce
2 tablespoons full cream or evaporated milk

Seasoning

pinch of celery salt or chopped celery
onion, finely chopped
lemon juice

METHOD

✿ To make the cocktail sauce, mix all the sauce ingredients
together in a bowl. Add seasoning and adjust if necessary.

✿ This dish can be arranged in glasses or small flat plates. Place
lettuce in cocktail dish and top with prawns, cover with sauce, and
garnish with lemon slices. Serve as cold as possible.

Bacon-wrapped Prawns

500 g prawns, peeled and deveined
6–8 rashers bacon, rind removed and rashers halved
bamboo skewers, soaked in water
60 g butter, melted
60 ml lemon juice

METHOD

✿ Wrap each prawn in a piece of bacon and thread onto bamboo skewers. In a small bowl or jug, combine melted butter and lemon juice. Brush over kebabs.

✿ Grill kebabs over hot coals for approximately 10–15 minutes, or until shrimp is cooked and bacon is lightly brown and crisp.

✿ Turn frequently while cooking, and brush again with the melted butter and lemon juice before serving. Serve any remaining butter with the kebabs.

Grilled Prawns

1 kg (2 lb) green prawns peeled and deveined

Marinade

250 ml olive oil
60 ml lemon juice
75g onion, finely chopped
2 cloves garlic, crushed
parsley, finely chopped
lemon and/or lime

METHOD

✿ To make marinade, place all marinade ingredients in a large bowl and mix well. Add prawns to the bowl and combine. Cover bowl and let stand for several hours in the refrigerator. Drain prawns.

✿ Place prawns in a heavy-based frying pan or on the bbq and cook on medium for 2–3 minutes, or until cooked and have changed colour.

✿ Stir frequently and add a little marinade while cooking.

✿ Serve immediately with some lemon and lime.

Garlic Prawns

SERVES 4–6

125 ml olive oil
4 large cloves garlic, peeled
1 tablespoon parsley, chopped
½ teaspoon salt
1 kg small green prawns peeled and deveined

METHOD

✿ In a bowl, combine oil, garlic, parsley and salt. Add prawns and let stand for 2 hours covered in the refrigerator.

✿ Preheat oven to 250°C.

✿ Place the prawns and marinade in an ovenproof casserole dish and cook in the oven for 10 minutes, or until prawns turn pink. Remove garlic cloves. Serve as an appetizer on small cocktail sticks, or as an entrée in small ramekins.

Chicken and Vegetable Soup

SERVES 4

1 kg chicken pieces, breasts and thighs
1 lemon, sliced
1 teaspoon salt
freshly ground black pepper
1 bay leaf
3 tablespoons medium-grain rice
2 carrots, thinly sliced
1 stalk celery, sliced
2 leeks, washed thoroughly and sliced, or 2 white onions, thinly
    sliced
¼ cup parsley, chopped

METHOD

✿ Where possible, remove skin from chicken. Pour over 8 cups cold water with lemon slices and allow to soak half an hour.

✿ Bring lemon water to boil. Add salt, pepper and bay leaf, then simmer for 30 minutes.

✿ Add rice and continue to cook for an extra 40 minutes. When chicken is quite tender, remove from broth. Remove any remaining chicken skin. Dice chicken into small pieces. Replace in broth, check seasoning, then cool and skim fat from broth. Reheat and serve sprinkled with parsley.

Tomato Soup

SERVES 4

750 g ripe tomatoes, chopped
1 potato, peeled and chopped
1 small onion, chopped
1 sprig fresh basil
1 teaspoon sugar
2 tablespoons tomato paste
salt and freshly ground black pepper
1 cup vegetable stock
¼ cup light whipping (thickened) cream
¼ cup parsley, finely chopped

METHOD

✿ Place all ingredients, except parsley and cream, into a saucepan with the stock. Bring to the boil and simmer, covered, for 20 minutes.

✿ Purée, then season with salt and pepper.

✿ Serve soup with a swirl of cream and sprinkle with chopped parsley.

Pea Soup

SERVES 4

250 g split peas
500 g bacon bones
1 litre cold water
2 carrots, roughly chopped
2 turnips, roughly chopped
2 onions, roughly chopped
4 stalks celery, chopped
salt and freshly ground black pepper
1 tablespoon all-purpose (plain) flour, mixed with 1 tablespoon
    water
croutons

METHOD

⚙ Wash peas and soak in water overnight. Place peas, water and bones in a saucepan and bring to the boil.

⚙ Add prepared vegetables and simmer for 1½ hours.

⚙ Remove bones, purée mixture, and season with salt and pepper. Thicken with flour paste and, stirring continuously, cook for 3 minutes. Garnish with croutons and serve immediately.

Smoked Oyster Dip

SERVES 2–4

125 g cream cheese
1 spring onion, cut into 25 mm lengths
1 teaspoon lemon juice
100 g canned smoked oysters
salt and freshly ground black pepper
1 packet crackers

METHOD

⚙ In a food processor, place cream cheese, spring onion and lemon juice and beat until smooth, with spring onion finely chopped.

⚙ Add smoked oysters with oil, directly from the can with salt and pepper. Pulse in 2 second bursts until oysters are roughly chopped.

⚙ Place in serving bowl, cover and refrigerate. Serve with a selection of crackers.

Oyster Kilpatrick

SERVES 4–6

12–24 oysters in the half shell
1 teaspoon Worcestershire sauce
1 cup cream
salt and freshly ground black pepper
250g (9 oz) bacon strips, finely chopped
fine bread crumbs

METHOD

✿ Remove oysters from shells and put aside.

✿ Put shells on a baking sheet and heat in a moderate oven. Mix Worcestershire sauce and cream.

✿ When shells are hot, return oysters to shells. Use tongs to handle the shells, as they get very hot.

✿ Add a little of the cream mixture to each shell and sprinkle with salt and pepper.

✿ Top each oyster with chopped bacon and fine breadcrumbs. Place under a hot grill and grill until bacon is crisp but not burnt and oysters are warmed through.

Note: Oysters Kilpatrick are very tasty served with a bowl of hot puréed spinach and thin slices of buttered brown or rye bread.

Oysters Natural

SERVES 1–2

12 oysters
lemon wedges

COCKTAIL SAUCE

2 tablespoons tomato ketchup
1 teaspoon Worcestershire sauce
2 teaspoons cream
pinch of ground black pepper

METHOD

❁ Arrange oysters on a bed of crushed ice with lemon wedges.

❁ Serve with chilled cocktail sauce in a small bowl in the centre of the plate.

❁ To make Cocktail Sauce, combine all ingredients together until well blended.

Oysters Mornay

SERVES 2–4

12 large, flat oysters
salt and pepper, to taste
1 tablespoon Parmesan cheese, grated

MORNAY SAUCE

15 g (½ oz) butter
1 tablespoon plain (all-purpose) flour
150 ml (5 fl oz) milk
60 g (2 oz) Gruyère cheese, grated
salt and freshly ground black pepper, to taste
1–2 tablespoons fresh cream

METHOD

✿ Sprinkle oysters with salt and pepper and place under a hot grill for 1 minute. Spread each oyster with mornay sauce to cover. Sprinkle with Parmesan cheese and bake in a hot oven for 5–10 minutes or until golden brown. Serve immediately.

✿ To make Mornay Sauce, melt butter in a small saucepan. Blend in flour until smooth, then cook for 1–2 minutes. Add milk and bring to the boil, stirring continuously. Remove pan from heat and add cheese. Stir until cheese melts. Season with salt and pepper and add enough cream to make the sauce a good coating consistency.

Oysters Greta Garbo

12 oysters in shells
juice of ½ lime or lemon
6 slices smoked salmon, cut into fine strips
1 cup sour cream
2 tablespoons fresh chives,
chopped, for garnish
red caviar for garnish
crushed ice for serving

METHOD

✿ Sprinkle the oysters with lime or lemon juice and top with smoked salmon.

✿ Put a dollop of the sour cream onto each oyster.

✿ Garnish with chives and red caviar.

✿ Serve on a bed of ice with a slice of lime.

Smoked Trout Pâté

SERVES 2–4

3 tablespoons butter
1 bunch chives, trimmed and snipped
2 smoked trout
3 hard-boiled eggs
1 teaspoon Thai sweet chili sauce
3 tablespoons good-quality mayonnaise
juice of 1 lemon
seeded lavash toast
6 pieces lavash bread
olive oil, for brushing
mixed seeds such as sesame and poppy

METHOD

⚙ Melt butter in a small saucepan over medium heat.

⚙ Add chives and cook for 1 minute, then remove from heat and set aside.

⚙ Remove skin from trout and carefully take flesh away from bone. Place trout, eggs, chili sauce, mayonnaise and lemon juice in a food processor and process until smooth. Season to taste with salt and pepper. Transfer to a bowl and fold in chive and butter mixture.

⚙ Refrigerate until ready to serve. Pâté can be made 1 day ahead. Keep covered in refrigerator. Serve chilled with seeded lavash toast.

To make seeded lavash toast:

❁ Preheat oven to 190°C.

❁ Cut lavash bread into triangles. Brush lightly with oil and place, oiled side up, in a single layer on parchment-lined (baking paper-lined) baking sheets.

❁ Sprinkle with seeds and/or cracked black pepper.

❁ Bake in preheated oven until golden, 6–8 minutes.

❁ Serve hot or cold.

Crumbed Calamari Rings

SERVES 2–4

750 g (1½ lb) squid tubes (squid hoods)
260 g (9 oz) plain (all-purpose) flour
sea salt and pepper
2–3 eggs
60 ml (2 fl oz) milk
120 g (4 oz) panko bread crumbs
oil, for deep-frying
lemon wedges, to serve

METHOD

✺ Cut squid tubes into 5 mm (¼ inch) rings. Place the rings on absorbent paper and dry well.

✺ Sift plain flour into a bowl and season with salt and pepper.

✺ Whisk eggs and milk together in a shallow bowl.

✺ Toss the squid rings into the flour, one at a time, then dip into the egg mixture, shaking off any extra liquid. Toss rings in panko breadcrumbs to coat. Heat oil to medium-high heat (it may spit and splatter, so be careful). Cook the rings in the hot oil until golden brown (3 minutes maximum). Drain well and serve hot with lemon wedges.

Damper

MAKES 1 LOAF

370 g plain flour
15 g butter
6 teaspoons baking powder
salt
water

METHOD

✿ In a bowl, rub the flour, butter, baking powder and salt together, until it is the texture of breadcrumbs.

✿ Make a well in the centre and add a little water. Mix into the flour and keep adding water until it is a firm dough. It will take about 45 minutes to cook. It is ready when the base is firm when tapped.

✿ Preheat the oven to 200°C and bake for 45–60 minutes. In a covered barbecue it will take about 10 minutes less, depending on how hot your fire is. Add chopped herbs to the mixture or use wholemeal flour, and milk instead of water.

✿ A handful or two of chopped dried fruit make a sweet addition.

Bacon and Egg Pie

SERVES 4

2 sheets puff pastry
1 medium brown onion (approximately 1 cup), finely chopped
125 g bacon, diced
2 tablespoons spicy chutney
6 medium eggs
salt and pepper
1 tablespoon milk
10 vine-ripened cherry tomatoes

METHOD

✿ Preheat oven to 200°C and grease an 20cm square oven-proof dish. Line the dish with 1 sheet of pastry.

✿ Sprinkle onion and bacon evenly over the pastry, then dot the chutney on top. Break eggs evenly over the top, pricking the yolks so they run slightly. Season with salt and pepper.

✿ Carefully position second sheet of pastry over filling, trim edges, and secure pastry by pressing down edges firmly using a fork. Brush pastry with milk.

✿ Bake for 40 minutes or until risen and golden.

✿ Serve hot or cold.

MAIN MEALS

Roast Beef

SERVES 4–6

1 x 1.5 kg rolled sirloin of beef
salt and freshly ground black pepper, to taste
butter or olive oil, for roasting
butchers string

METHOD

⚙ Preheat oven to 165°C.

⚙ Rub meat with salt and pepper and place in a roasting pan, fat side up. If the joint has little fat, add 1–2 tablespoons butter or oil to the pan.

⚙ Tie string around the meat to hold it together.

⚙ Place beef in the oven and cook for 2 hours.

⚙ Remove roast beef to a hot carving platter and leave to stand in a warm place for 15–30 minutes before carving. This makes it easier to carve the meat. Serve with roast vegetables (pumpkin or parsnip, potatoes, carrots), and with your choice of gravy or horseradish cream or mustard.

T-bone Steak

SERVES 4

4 T-bone steaks, about 300 g each
olive oil
salt and freshly ground black pepper

METHOD

⚙ Take out T-bones and let them come to room temperature.

⚙ Brush the steaks with olive oil and season with salt and pepper.

⚙ Cook the steaks on the barbecue grill or a hot pan on the stove top for 3 minutes each side or until cooked to your liking.

⚙ Serve the steaks with crispy potatoes or a salad.

Steak Sandwich

SERVES 2

500 g rump or sirloin steak
(whichever you prefer)
pepper, freshly ground, to taste
salt, to taste

Sandwich
loaf of sliced sourdough
cup of rocket
2 tomatoes, sliced
caramelised onion, to serve
mayonnaise, to serve

METHOD

✿ Prepare barbecue for direct heat cooking on a high or cook on your frypan.

✿ Season the steak with salt and pepper on both sides place the steak on the grill and cook to your liking.

✿ Rest the steak while you toast sourdough on the grill. Slice the steak then butter one side of the toasted sourdough. Add the mayonnaise, rocket and tomato the season with salt and pepper to taste and top with the sliced steak and caramelised onion. Place the other slice of sourdough on top and enjoy.

Meat Pie

SERVES 4

2 tablespoons oil
1 kg chuck or skirt steak, cut into 2.5 cm cubes
2 onions, chopped
½ cup celery, chopped
½ cup carrot, chopped
500 ml (1 pint) beef stock
2 teaspoons salt
¼ teaspoon freshly
ground black pepper
¼ teaspoon
ground nutmeg
3 tablespoons plain
(all-purpose) flour
185 g short crust pastry
1 egg, beaten, for glazing

METHOD

✿ Heat oil in a large saucepan and fry steak in about three lots until browned, then remove.

✿ Add onion, celery and carrot and cook for a few minutes. Replace meat, add stock, cover and simmer gently for 1 hour. Add salt, pepper and nutmeg and simmer for another hour, until cooked.

✿ In a cup, blend flour with a little cold water to form a smooth paste. Add to saucepan and cook a little longer, until mixture thickens. Taste and adjust flavour.

✿ Preheat oven to 200°C.

✿ Roll out pastry on a lightly floured board, so that it is 2.5 cm larger than the top of the pie dish. Cut a strip 1 cm wide off the edge and place it on the dampened edge of the pie dish.

✿ Glaze this strip of pastry with egg, then roll out remaining pastry for lid, easing it gently. (If you stretch it, it will shrink during cooking.)

✿ Press edges together, then trim combined edge and decorate with a knife. Glaze pastry with egg.

✿ Make a few holes in the pastry for steam to escape.

✿ Bake in the oven for 25 minutes, or until cooked.

Sausage Rolls

MAKES 24 SMALL SAUSAGE ROLLS

4 flaky pastry sheets
500 g (1 lb) sausage meat or mince beef or lamb
beaten egg, for glazing

METHOD

✿ Preheat oven to 220°C.

✿ Divide pastry in half.

✿ Cut each half into a 7.5 x 30 cm strip.

✿ Form sausage meat into 2 rolls, each 30 cm (12 in) long.
Lay a sausage meat or mince and roll close to the edge of each
pastry strip.

✿ Dampen one side of pastry with water, then fold pastry over
and press edges together firmly.

✿ Glaze tops of long sausage roll with beaten egg then cut each
roll into 12 pieces.

✿ Place rolls on a baking tray and bake in the oven for
15 minutes. Reduce oven temperature to moderately hot (200°C)
and bake for a further 10–15 minutes.

Marinated Barbecue Pork Chops

SERVES 4

4 pork chops

Marinade

3 tablespoons soy sauce

3 tablespoons Worcestershire sauce

3 tablespoons hoisin barbecue sauce

1 tablespoon balsamic vinegar

1 teaspoon garlic powder

1 teaspoon onion powder

salt and pepper, to taste

METHOD

⬡ Trim the pork chops of rind and excess fat.

⬡ Place all the marinade ingredients into a large zip-lock bag. Add the pork chops and marinade for 1–2 hours or longer if possible.

⬡ Heat the barbecue grill, then cook the chops for 5–6 minutes on each side. For crosshatch grill marks, turn 45 degrees after 3 minutes.

⬡ Turn down the grill and baste with the leftover marinade until the chops are cooked through.

⬡ When done, cover with foil and rest for 5 minutes before serving.

Corned Silverside with White Sauce

SERVES 4

1.5–2 kg piece of corned silverside
1 tablespoon brown sugar
12 whole black peppercorns
1 bay leaf
1 tablespoon vinegar
vegetables of your choice
parsley sprigs, to garnish

METHOD

✿ Place silverside in a deep saucepan and cover with cold water. Add remaining ingredients.

✿ Bring to simmering point and cook, covered, for 2 hours.

✿ Garnish with sprigs of parsley, and serve your choose of vegetables and white sauce.

✿ NOTE: Corned silverside can also be served cold.

✿ Allow to cool in the cooking liquid, and when cold, wrap in plastic clingwrap or aluminium foil and store in the refrigerator.

White sauce

30 g butter
30 g plain flour
1¼ cups milk
salt and freshly ground black pepper, to taste

METHOD

✿ Melt butter in a saucepan over a low heat, then remove from heat and stir in flour.

✿ Return to heat and cook gently for a few minutes, making sure that the roux does not brown.

✿ Remove pan from heat and gradually blend in cold milk.

✿ Replace pan on heat and bring to the boil. Reduce heat and cook, stirring with a wooden spoon, until smooth. Season well. If any lumps have formed, whisk briskly.

Shepherd's Pie

SERVES 4

1 tablespoon olive oil
1 large onion, chopped
1 clove garlic, crushed
500 g minced lamb
400 g jar tomato and basil pasta sauce
2 tablespoons chopped fresh parsley
2 teaspoons red wine vinegar
salt and freshly ground black pepper
680 g potatoes, peeled and chopped
250 g carrots, chopped
60 g butter

METHOD

⚙ Heat the oil in a large frying pan, cook the onion and garlic over a medium heat for 5 minutes, until softened. Increase the heat slightly and add the mince.

⚙ Fry for a further 5 minutes, breaking up any lumps with a wooden spoon, until the meat has browned.

⚙ Stir in the sauce, together with the parsley, vinegar and seasoning. Simmer, covered, for about 20 minutes, stirring occasionally.

⚙ Meanwhile, cook the potatoes and carrots in boiling, salted water for 15–20 minutes, until tender.

⚙ Drain, then mash the potatoes with the butter and season with pepper.

❁ Preheat the oven to 190°C.

❁ Transfer the mince to a large, shallow, ovenproof dish.

❁ Spoon over the mashed potato topping in an even layer and fluff up with a fork.

❁ Cook for 35–40 minutes, until the potato is browned. Serve with the carrots on the side.

Lamb Rissoles

SERVES 2-4

500 g (18 oz) lamb mince
1 small onion finely diced
45 g (1½ fl oz) breadcrumbs
30 g (1 oz) diced sweet chargrilled capsicum
1 egg
1 clove garlic finely chopped
1 teaspoon ground cumin
¼ bunch fresh mint, finely chopped (keep some for garnish)
spray oil for cooking

METHOD

⚙ Place the mince, onion, breadcrumbs, mint, garlic and cumin in the bowl and combine. Season with salt and pepper.

⚙ Divide mince mixture into 6 portions the shape each portion into a patty.

⚙ Heat barbecue plate or chargrill over medium–low heat.

⚙ Spray both sides of rissoles with oil.

⚙ Cook, turning occasionally, for 12 to 15 minutes or until cooked through.

⚙ Serve on platter with a salad or make a burger.

Leg of Lamb Roast

SERVES 4

1½ kg leg of lamb
2 cloves garlic, cut into slivers
2 fresh rosemary sprigs, cut into small pieces
salt and black pepper
whole potatoes
300 g carrots, chopped
vegetable oil
1¼ cups red wine
2 tablespoons of red wine vinegar

METHOD

✿ Preheat the oven to 180°C. Make several incisions in the lamb
using a sharp knife. Push the garlic slivers and pieces of rosemary
into the incisions, then season well.

✿ Rub some vegetable oil onto the roast with salt and pepper as
desired. Arrange the potatoes and carrots in a large roasting tin and
place the lamb on top. Pour in the wine and vinegar and roast for
2–2½ hours until the lamb is tender, basting the lamb and turning
the vegetables every 30 minutes. Add a little more wine or water if
necessary.

✿ Transfer the lamb to a plate, then cover with foil and rest for
15 minutes. Carve the lamb and serve with the vegetables.

Grilled Lamb Cutlets

SERVES 2

6 lamb cutlets
salt and freshly ground black pepper, to taste
olive oil for frying

METHOD

⚙ Trim cutlets of excess fat and season well on each side. Put on rack in grill pan, and brush with oil.

⚙ Cook under a very hot grill for 2 minutes to sear meat. Turn and sear other side for 2 minutes.

⚙ Reduce the heat and cook for a further 10 minutes (turning once after 5 minutes), or until cooked.

⚙ Serve with salad or vegetables.

Chicken Rissoles

SERVES 4

500 g minced chicken
½ teaspoon salt
½ teaspoon freshly ground black pepper
30 g dried breadcrumbs
1 medium onion, finely chopped
2 tablespoons finely chopped fresh parsley
juice of ½ lemon
1 egg
1 tablespoon oil
60 g plain flour

METHOD

⚙ In a large bowl, add the mince,salt, pepper, breadcrumbs, onion, parsley, lemon juice and egg. Combine well with a wooden spoon and cover bowl and rest in the fridge for 20 minutes.

⚙ With wet hands, shape a heaped tablespoon of rissole mixture into an oval shape and flatten with palm of hand. Repeat with remaining mixture.

⚙ Mix the flour with desired amount of salt and pepper.
Coat each rissole in seasoned flour, shake off excess and place in hot oil.

⚙ Heat oil in a large wok or frying pan. Cook for 4 minutes on each side. When cooked drain on absorbent paper.

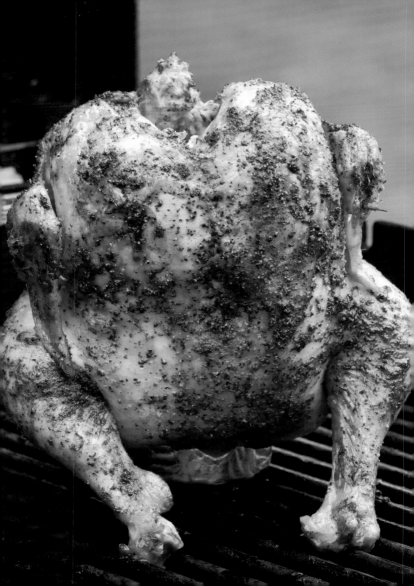

Sticky Beer Can Chicken

SERVES 4

1 large whole chicken
1 teaspoon vegetable oil
¼ teaspoon pepper
½ teaspoon sea salt
½ teaspoon chicken spice rub
1 can beer (or soft drink can may also be used)
2 tablespoons barbecue sauce

METHOD

✿ Dry chicken with a paper towel to absorb any moisture. Rub the chicken inside and out with vegetable oil. Season with salt, pepper and spice rub. Open the beer can and pour out ½ of the liquid. Place the can on a cutting board and lower the chicken on to the can so it looks like it is sitting on it. Position the legs like a tripod so the chicken sits upright.

✿ Place the chicken in the middle of the barbecue and close lid. Cook the chicken for about a 1 hour or until golden brown.

✿ The chicken is done when the juices run clear when skewer is pushed into thickest part of the thigh. Brush the chicken with barbecue sauce and cook for a further 10 minutes until dark and sticky.

Roast Chicken

SERVES 6

1 x 1.5 kg chicken, washed and dried
salt and freshly ground black pepper, to taste
3 tablespoons olive oil
315 ml chicken stock

METHOD

⚜ Preheat oven to 180°C.

⚜ Rub chicken with salt, pepper and half the olive oil.

⚜ Truss chicken and place in a greased roasting pan with remaining oil.

⚜ Cook in the oven, basting occasionally, for 1 hour, or until tender and golden brown all over.

⚜ Remove chicken and keep warm.

⚜ While chicken is cooking make chicken stock.

⚜ Add chicken stock to pan juices and bring to the boil.

⚜ Strain into a sauceboat and serve with chicken, roast potatoes and green vegetables.

SEAFOOD

Lobster Mornay

SERVES 2

1 medium lobster, cooked and halved
1¼ cups milk
1 bay leaf
1 small onion, chopped
5 black peppercorns
30 g butter
2 tablespoons plain flour
60 ml cream
60 g tasty cheese, grated
salt and freshly ground black pepper
1 tablespoon butter, extra
60 g fresh breadcrumbs
chopped parsley

METHOD

✿ Remove the lobster meat from the shells and cut into bite-size pieces.

✿ Reserve the shells. In a saucepan, place the milk, bay leaf, onion and peppercorns. Heat slowly to boiling point. Remove from heat, cover and let stand for 10 minutes. Strain.

✿ In a pan, heat the butter, and remove from the heat.

✿ Stir in the flour and blend, gradually adding the strained milk. Return the pan to the heat, and stir constantly until the sauce boils and thickens. Simmer the sauce for 1 minute. Remove from the heat and add the cream, cheese, salt and pepper. Stir the sauce until cheese melts, then add the lobster.

✲ Divide the mixture between the shells. Melt the extra butter in a small pan, add two-thirds of the breadcrumbs, and stir to combine.

✲ Scatter the remaining breadcrumbs over the lobster and brown under a hot grill.

✲ Sprinkle chopped parsley and serve hot.

Grilled Flathead

SERVES 4

4 flathead (500–600 g each)
2 tablespoons sumac spice
4 tablespoons olive oil bunch of fresh dill
2 lemons
8–12 wooden skewers, soaked for 30 minutes

METHOD

⚙ Clean and gut the fish and remove the head. Cut off the fins and trim the tail with a pair of kitchen scissors. In a small bowl mix together the olive oil and the sumac. Slice the lemons. Wash the dill and trim off the stalks.

⚙ Place the fish on their backs on a chopping board.

⚙ Into each fish cavity place a good handful of dill and 2–3 slices of lemon, then pour on some of the oil and sumac mix.

⚙ With 2–3 small wooden skewers, fasten together the fish so the dill and lemon do not fall out during cooking.

⚙ Turn the fish over and rub the oil and sumac mix well into the fish. Prepare the barbecue for direct-heat cooking. Oil the grill bars well. Cook the fish on each side for 8–10 minutes.

Grilled Scampi with Herb Butter

SERVES 6

10–12 scampi
140 g butter
few sprigs fresh herbs (parsley, coriander and thyme), chopped
2 tablespoons chopped fresh parsley
2 cloves garlic, finely chopped
salt and freshly ground black pepper

METHOD

✿ Split the scampi lengthwise through the centre and arrange, cut side up, on a large shallow dish. Melt the butter and add the herbs and garlic.

✿ Drizzle the flavoured butter over the scampi and season with pepper. (The scampi can be prepared ahead up to this stage.)

✿ Preheat the griller and arrange the scampi, cut side up, on the grilling pan. Cook for about 5 minutes until the flesh has turned white.

✿ Remove from the heat, season with salt and arrange on a large serving platter with wedges of lime. To eat the scampi use a fork to pull out the tail meat. Place a bowl on the table for the discarded shells, and a few fingerbowls, each with a squeeze of lemon.

Barbecued Whole Snapper

SERVES 4–6

1 whole snapper, about 1½ kg
½ red capsicum, chopped
¼ cup fresh basil, chopped
2 tablespoons lemon juice
1 tablespoon olive oil

METHOD

✿ Scale the fish and rinse well. Pat dry with paper towels. Mix the capsicum, basil, lemon juice and oil together. Spoon some into the cavity and spread the remainder over the fish.

✿ Lay the fish on a large sheet of oiled foil and roll up the edges to form an enclosure around the fish. Place on a wire cake rack and place the rack on top of the grill bars, elevating so the fish is 10 cm above the source of heat.

✿ Cook for 10–12 minutes on each side.

✿ Turn carefully using a large spatula, or place the fish in a hinged fish rack and turn when needed. Serve fish while hot.

Scampi with Basil Butter

SERVES 2–4

8 uncooked scampi or yabbies, heads removed
basil butter
85g (3 oz) butter, melted
2 tablespoons chopped fresh basil
1 clove garlic, crushed
2 teaspoons honey

METHOD

✿ Cut the scampi or yabbies in half, lengthwise.

✿ To make the basil butter, place the butter, basil, garlic and honey in a small bowl and whisk to combine.

✿ Brush the cut side of each scampi or yabbie half with basil butter and cook under a preheated hot grill for 2 minutes or until the shells turn red and are tender.

✿ Drizzle with any remaining basil butter and serve immediately.

SIDES

Barbecue Potatoes

SERVES 4–6

4–6 medium sized potatoes, washed
1 tablespoon oil
1 teaspoon salt

METHOD

✿ Place the washed potatoes in a bowl. Combine the oil and salt, pour over potatoes and toss to coat. Wrap each potato in a piece of foil.

✿ Place potatoes on the barbecue grill as soon as you light the barbecue. The potatoes will heat and get a head start before it is hot enough to cook the meat.

✿ Turn the potatoes at times. When barbecue heats up, turn the potatoes more frequently.

✿ Test with a skewer. If soft, remove and keep warm.

✿ Potatoes will take about 20 minutes with the slow start.

✿ Fold the foil back from the potatoes. Cut a cross in the top and squeeze from the base to open out.

Add a good dollop of sour cream or butter.

Cauliflower Cheese

SERVES 4

500 g cauliflower, cut into small pieces
¼ cup fresh breadcrumbs
¼ small bunch flat-leaf parsley

CHEESE SAUCE

30 g butter
¼ cup all-purpose (plain) flour
1¼ cups milk, warmed
1 teaspoon wholegrain mustard
80 g Parmesan cheese, grated, at room temperature
salt
white pepper

METHOD

✿ Lightly butter a heatproof dish. Cook the cauliflower in a saucepan of lightly salted boiling water for 8 minutes or until just tender. Drain thoroughly, then transfer to the prepared dish and keep warm.

✿ To make the cheese sauce, melt the butter in a pan over low heat. Stir in the flour and cook for 1 minute, or until lightly coloured and bubbling. Remove from the heat and gradually stir in the milk and mustard.

✿ If lumps form, press the mixture through a strainer. Return to the heat and stir constantly until the sauce simmers and thickens. Reduce the heat and simmer for a further 2 minutes, then remove from the heat again.

✿ Add the Parmesan and stir until thoroughly combined. Season with salt and white pepper and pour over the cauliflower.

✿ Combine the breadcrumbs and parsley and sprinkle evenly on top of the sauce. Grill under a medium heat until the top is golden brown. Serve immediately.

Barbecued Smashed Baby Potatoes

SERVES 4–6

1 kg new baby potatoes
2 tablespoons olive oil
salt, to season
2 tablespoons rosemary and garlic seasoning

METHOD

⚙ Add the whole baby potatoes to a large saucepan of salted water over medium heat.

⚙ Bring to the boil, then reduce to a simmer. Cook for about 20 minutes, or until a fork can be pushed through with no resistance.

⚙ Drain the potatoes. Once they are cool enough to handle, place on a chopping board and smash each potato.

⚙ Place in a large bowl, and dress with the olive oil, salt and seasoning. Place the potatoes on a hot barbecue grill and cook for about 5 minutes on each side, or until lightly browned and crisp.

⚙ Remove the potatoes to a platter, sprinkle with the remaining rosemary and garlic seasoning and serve immediately.

Rosemary and Garlic Seasoning

5 g dried rosemary

2 teaspoons garlic powder

2 teaspoons onion powder

1 teaspoon black peppercorns

1 teaspoon salt

METHOD

✿ Using a mortar and pestle, spice grinder or coffee grinder, grind the rosemary and peppercorn into a powder.

✿ In a small bowl, combine all of the ingredients.

✿ Note: Store in an airtight container for up to 6 months.

Corn on the Cob

SERVES 4

4 cobs of corn
30 g butter, melted, plus extra to serve
salt and freshly ground black pepper, to taste
parsley chopped

METHOD

✿ Strip the silk off the corn. Brush the corn with melted butter and sprinkle with salt and freshly ground black pepper.

✿ Replace the husks and secure in three places with string.

✿ Barbecue the corn cobs over hot grill for 15–20 minutes, or until tender, turning frequently.

✿ When cooked, the husks will be dry and brown and the corn will be golden brown. Serve with melted butter and salt and pepper and sprinkle chopped parsley.

No matter where you visit throughout Australia's country communities, you will always see the joys of homemade produce shining through.

Australians take great pride in sharing their tasty offerings, and recipes are often passed from one generation to the next.

Summer-season fruit like raspberries and strawberries are over so quickly, but by making the fruit into jam you can capture the flavour to provide delicious year-round enjoyment.

Farmers' lunch sandwiches are spread with tasty cheese and chutneys. The results of home pickling are invariably tastier and cheaper than commercial varieties, and you can cut costs by buying produce when there is a glut and prices are down.

JAMS AND PRESERVES

Strawberry Jam

2 kg granulated sugar
2 kg strawberries, hulled
juice and rind of 2 lemons

METHOD

⚙ Warm the sugar in a slow oven. Put the strawberries and lemon in a saucepan and heat gently, stirring as the juice begins to flow out of the fruit. When the juice is coming to the boil, add the warmed sugar.

⚙ After it has dissolved, bring the jam to a rapid boil until it thickens and reaches the setting point (about 15–20 minutes). Remove from the heat and let stand for 15 minutes. Ladle into sterilised jars, label and seal.

⚙ A perennial favourite, strawberry jam tastes delicious with warm fresh croissants and tea.

Apricot Jam

200 g dried apricots
3 cups water
2 tablespoons lemon juice
625 g granulated sugar

METHOD

⚙ Place the apricots in a strainer and rinse under running water.

⚙ Place in a bowl, add the water and allow to soak for several hours or overnight.

⚙ Place the apricots and soaking water in a saucepan. Bring to the boil, turn down the heat to moderate, cover and cook for 20 minutes, until the apricots are very soft.

⚙ Add the lemon juice and sugar; stir until all the sugar is dissolved. Reduce the heat and simmer, uncovered, until the setting point is reached (about 30 minutes).

⚙ Stir occasionally to make sure the jam is not catching on the bottom (jam may be cooked more rapidly, but it is more likely to catch on the bottom). As soon as the setting point is reached, remove from the heat. Allow to cool enough to place in warm, sterilised jars. Label and seal.

Orange Marmalade

1 kg Seville oranges
juice of 1 lemon
8 cups water
2 kg granulated sugar

METHOD

✹ Cut the oranges in half and squeeze out the juice. Strain the juice into a saucepan. Cut the peel finely, and put the pips into a muslin bag.

✹ Combine the juice and rind of the oranges with the lemon juice, the bag of pips and the water in the saucepan. Bring slowly to the boil and simmer for up to 2 hours or until the rind is tender. Add the sugar and stir until it has dissolved. Take out the muslin bag and squeeze the pectin back into the marmalade.

✹ Bring to the boil and boil rapidly for about 10 minutes or until the setting point is reached.

✹ Remove from the heat, let the marmalade rest for 30 minutes, stir the fruit gently, and spoon into sterilised jars. Label and seal when cold.

Dried Fig Jam

1 kg dried figs, roughly chopped
8 cups water
rind, pips and juice of 2 lemons
1 teaspoon fennel seeds
3 tablespoons pine nuts
60 g flaked almonds
750 g granulated sugar

METHOD

⚙ Soak the dried figs in 1 litre of water for several hours.

⚙ Put the lemon rind and pips into a muslin bag. Place the figs, remaining water, lemon juice and bag of rind and pips in a saucepan and bring to the boil. Simmer until the figs are tender, stirring constantly.

⚙ Add the fennel seeds, pine nuts, flaked almonds and sugar, then stir until the sugar dissolves. Squeeze the juice out of the muslin bag into the jam and discard the bag. Boil, stirring constantly, until the setting point is reached. Ladle the jam into warm sterilised jars. Label and seal.

Tomato Chutney

2 kg tomatoes, peeled and roughly chopped
20 cloves garlic, roughly chopped
2 tablespoons chopped fresh ginger
90 g raisins
370 g granulated sugar
1 tablespoon salt
2 chillies
rind and juice of 1 lemon
½ teaspoon cumin seeds
½ teaspoon fennel seeds
½ teaspoon fenugreek
1½ cups white wine vinegar

METHOD

✿ Combine all the ingredients in a saucepan, bring to the boil, and simmer for 1½–2 hours, stirring frequently, or until the chutney is thick.

✿ The cooking time depends on how firm the tomatoes are; if they are watery, it will take longer to cook. Spoon into sterilised jars, seal, and store in a dark, dry cupboard.

BAKES

Scones

MAKES 10–12

2 cups self-raising flour
1 teaspoon baking powder
2 teaspoons sugar
45 g butter
1 egg
½ cup milk

METHOD

⚙ Preheat the oven to 220°C. Sift together flour and baking powder into a large bowl. Stir in sugar, then rub in butter, using fingertips, until mixture resembles coarse breadcrumbs.

⚙ Whisk together egg and milk. Make a well in the centre of the flour mixture, pour in egg mixture and mix to form a soft dough. Turn onto a lightly floured surface and knead lightly.

⚙ Press dough out to a 2cm thickness, using palm of hand.

⚙ Cut out scones using a floured 5cm cutter. Avoid twisting the cutter, or the scones will rise unevenly.

⚙ Arrange scones close together on a greased and lightly floured baking tray or in a shallow 20cm round cake tin.

⚙ Brush with a little milk and bake for 12–15 minutes or until golden.

⚙ Serve with jam and cream fresh out of the oven.

Lamingtons

MAKES 10–12

1 pre-baked butter or sponge cake, 18 x 28cm
500 g icing sugar
3 tablespoons cocoa powder
6–8 tablespoons warm water
500 g desiccated coconut

METHOD

⊛ Cut sponge into 12 squares. Set aside.

⊛ Place icing sugar and cocoa powder in sifter or sieve.

⊛ Sift into large bowl.

⊛ Stir in water until you have a runny icing. Pour icing into one of the shallow cake tins. Place coconut in the other tin.

⊛ Using tongs or 2 forks dip cake squares in chocolate icing. Remove cake from icing. Allow excess icing to drain off. Roll in coconut. Place lamingtons on wire rack to set.

Fruit Cake

2 cups dried mixed fruit
150 g butter
½ cup brown sugar
1 teaspoon mixed spice
1 cup orange juice
2 eggs
1¾ cups plain flour
3 teaspoons baking powder

METHOD

⚙ Preheat the oven to 150°C. Place mixed fruit, butter, brown sugar, mixed spice and orange juice in a saucepan large enough to mix all the ingredients.

⚙ Heat, stirring until boiling. Boil for 4 minutes. Leave to cool.

⚙ Using a wooden spoon, beat in eggs, flour and baking powder until combined. Spoon into a 20cm round cake tin lined with baking paper.

⚙ Bake for 1–1¼ hours or until a skewer comes out clean. Leave in tin for 10 minutes before turning on to a wire rack.

Chocolate Cake

½ cup butter, softened

2 cups caster sugar

2 eggs

2 teaspoons vanilla extract

1½ cups plain flour

1¾ teaspoons baking powder

5 tablespoons cocoa powder

1 cup buttermilk

Chocolate Sour-Cream Filling

1¼ cups bittersweet chocolate, broken into pieces

½ cup chopped butter

3 cups icing sugar, sifted

½ cup sour cream

1 cup raspberry jam

METHOD

✿ Preheat the oven to 180°C. Place the butter, caster sugar, eggs, and vanilla extract in a bowl and beat until light and fluffy. Sift together the flour, baking powder and cocoa powder.

✿ Fold the flour mixture and the buttermilk, alternately, into the butter mixture. Divide the mixture between 4 greased and lined 23 cm round cake pans and bake for 25 minutes or until the cakes are cooked when tested with a skewer. Turn cakes onto wire racks to cool.

✿ To make the filling, place the chocolate and butter in a heatproof bowl set over a saucepan of simmering water and heat, stirring, until the mixture is smooth.

✿ Remove the bowl from the pan. Add the icing sugar and sour cream and mix until smooth.

✿ To assemble the cake, place 1 cake on a serving plate, spread with the jam and top with some filling. Top with a second cake, some more jam and some filling. Repeat the layers to use all the cakes and jam. Finish with a layer of cake and spread the remaining filling over the top and sides of the cake.

Index

First published in 2025 by New Holland Publishers
Sydney

Level 1, 178 Fox Valley Road, Wahroonga, NSW 2076, Australia

newhollandpublishers.com

A record of this book is held at the National Library of Australia.

ISBN 9781760797737

Managing Director: Fiona Schultz
General Manager/Publisher: Olga Dementiev
Designer: Andrew Davies
Production Director: Arlene Gippert
Printed in China

Keep up with New Holland Publishers:

[f] NewHollandPublishers
[◎] @newhollandpublishers